Sally MacKinnon Consulting
Your Fitness Friend
The Mermaid Surf Yoga Academy
37 Bibaringa Close Beechmont Queensland Australia 4211
salmackinnon@bigpond.com
yourfitnessfriendgc.blogspot.com.au

First published 2016
ISBN: 978-0-646-95555-1

Design: Artisans Graphic Art Studio   Printing: IngramSpark

the dharma of surfing

wisdom from the water for life

Sally MacKinnon

with Scott Johnson and Huon MacKinnon-Farnworth

the dharma of surfing

wisdom from the water for life

For me personally I'm interested in the idea of surfing with a pure heart. Because when your heart is open and receptive to an intimacy with the sea, a wealth of gifts can be discovered. A surfing life can impart so much: patience, humility, wisdom, an understanding of the significance of beauty, the desire for wildness, the connection to place, a sense of belonging in the world, the appreciation of the value of pure, simple joy.

So for me, why you surf is more important than how you surf. I'm intrigued in the ideal of surfers who are so enchanted by the sea, who are so grateful for the gift of wave-riding, who are so affected by the exchange, that they're actually upon the journey of becoming seaworthy.

Nathan Oldfield

There is a language older by far and deeper than words. It is the language of bodies, of body on body, wind on snow, rain on trees, wave on stone. It is a language of dreams, of gesture, of symbol, of memory. We have forgotten this language, forgotten it for so long we do not even remember it exists. If we are to survive, we must again remember this language. We must learn to think like the planet.

Derrick Jensen

gazing out to sea...

Surfing is more than standing up on a surfboard. It is, I believe, the language of 'Oceanspeak'; of feet on waves, of heart in sky, of breath and body in synch with Mother Nature.

When I finally had my first surf lesson on my 46th birthday, before we were even in the water, I was enamoured by the instructor's description of how waves work, where and why they break, how they move and how to catch their foaming, rolling, powerful energy.

Then, when I stood up on the long, wide foam board in that first lesson and felt the waves bear my weight across the top of the water towards the beach, I heard the surf gods shout from the heavens "You will be a surfer" and I knew nothing would ever be the same again.

Surfing saved my life. I was so instantly and utterly absorbed with riding waves and being in the ocean for hours at a time, that I stopped being a workaholic in a job that was breaking my heart and drowning my spirit.

I made time in my busy family and work life to surf many times a week. Within a few years I completely changed my career largely so I could surf more and feel the joy and playfulness of it all.

I connected with complete abandon (and sometimes with a little fear) to the natural elements. To the sea, the sky, the sand, the wind, the tides, the rocky headlands and all the creatures that live within them.

I came home to Mother Nature and to myself.

When I became a surf instructor at the age of 50 and began introducing people to the sea and the waves and the winds and the tides and how to surrender to those forces in order to ride a surfboard in harmony with them, I realised that surfing and those elements were my dearest teachers.

I began to jot down all the lessons I was learning and how they illuminated and supported my life on land as well as in the water.

I also realised there were other surfers who felt the same way I did; who surfed from the heart and the soul in communion with the sea. Soul surfers and storytellers like Nathan Oldfield whose beautiful quote from his film "Seaworthy" begins this book. Surfers who feel that why we surf is more important than how we surf in our journeys toward becoming pure-hearted and worthy of the sea.

And so *"the dharma of surfing"* was born. The word 'dharma' has many meanings for Hindus, Buddhists and Jains and there is apparently, no clear single word for it in Western languages. Vietnamese Buddhist monk, poet and peacemaker Thich Nhat Hanh describes Dharma as "the Way of Understanding and Love" (The Heart of the Buddha's Teaching, 1998, p7) and in everyday terms we might think of dharma as 'right way of living' or 'path of connection and compassion' where the way we behave helps support personal and universal coherence.

I'd like to think that if we surf with a spirit of sharing, connection, love, mindfulness, gratitude, humility, joyfulness, awareness, playfulness and curiosity then we might also take those qualities and behaviours further into our lives as a right way of living.

Thank you to all who are curious to explore this book with its simple words and beautiful photographs. There are 52 wisdoms and images – one for each week of the year – if you like to play this way.

Thank you to Huon MacKinnon-Farnworth and Scott Johnson, collaborating photographers, for their generous support and illuminating images.

Thank you to Garry and Kandy Palmer from Surf Easy Surf School at Currumbin Alley – my friends, surfing mentors and employers – for opening the door to the happiest life ever.

Thank you to all the Surf Easy Surf School students I have worked with and the Currumbin Alley Mermaids and Foresthaven Soul-Surfing Mermaids who are such a huge part of my surfing life.

Thank you Mother Nature for your abundant gifts.

Sal

In surfing and in life, where you look and what you look at is where you'll go. Look down and you'll nose dive or fall. Look along the line of the wave as you paddle into it and take off, and that's where you'll dance with Mother Nature. What you see is what you'll get, so look for the beauty and give thanks.

Before paddling out or stepping into your day, take some time to stand still, feel your feet on the earth, observe the conditions, breathe in time with the ocean, give thanks and form your intentions for your practice. There's no need to rush. Time spent synchronising is time well spent.

Remember the Aloha spirit: share the waves; respect the land, sea, sky and fellow surfers; offer your thanks to Mother Nature; breathe peace; help create public spaces that are safe for everyone; leave only footprints.

Never try to fight or control a wave. It is a far greater force than we will ever be. Welcome its energy into your life, go with its flow and learn humility and grace as you dance across it with Mother Nature. She is our greatest teacher.

Dynamic balance is a foundation of surfing and of life. Find your feet on the board or on the earth, follow your breath and feel the stillness in action and the action in stillness. Sometimes you have to work for your balance. Always you have to find a drishti, a point of focus, a gaze point that helps you to commit and fly.

There is no time-constrained destination in surfing or in life. These are our practices, works in progress, lifelong journeys and labours of love. Surrender to their grace and illumination without expectations of achievements. Learn to love the unfolding of your skills and growth to the rhythms of Mother Nature and the cosmos.

Things that seem impossible in the beginning: standing on a surfboard and riding waves, surfing out the back, or catching barrels for example, are part of an ever-unfolding story without timelines or expectations. If we turn up every day to participate wholeheartedly, without tight expectations of what we should be doing or achieving, then we will begin to create a groove in our lives that is more gentle and tuned to the rhythms of the cosmos.

With gratitude for each breath, each wave and each surf, the 'impossibles' will smile at us and gracefully appear in their own good time. We will blossom by simply turning up.

When you feel anxious and begin to touch the far edges of your comfort and security in the surf and in life, deepen the fluttery shallow breath that accompanies those feelings by drawing it deeply down into the belly when you breathe in. Then feel the outbreath move out of your body and hover for just a moment before the next deep inhale begins. Keep breathing deeply in and out, in and out.

There you will find calm courage and the depth of presence to stay with and explore those edges.

When you see a wave you want to catch in the big blue and in life, paddle into it with unwavering commitment and strength, look in the direction you want to go, let the wave's momentum gather you up, trust your body to do what it knows, then feel your feet on the board and go with that flow.

There are forces far greater than us and when we surf, we can move with those forces for the rides of our lives.

In Yoga there is a profoundly simple and deep posture called Mountain pose — Tadasana. When we stand in it we feel every part of our feet on the ground, on the Earth and as we inhale we breathe Mother Earth's energy up through our entire body. When we exhale we connect with Father Sky through the crown of our head. We stand still with our arms to our sides, our palms open and we release everything we are hanging on to through our fingertips. Then we feel the stillness, patience and timelessness of the mountain.

When you surf then, take the stability of Tadasana into the water with you. Feel every part of your feet and toes on the surfboard and on the wave. Connect totally with Mother Nature and feel her joy, generosity, wisdom, stability and power surge through you.

You can turn a marginal surf session or a difficult day around by following your breath, refocusing your attention and finding grace. You can change your energy and the energy around you with just a few deep, slow breaths and a shift of perspective that notices the good things, the positives, and gives thanks. Then feel the change wash through you like an incoming tide and smile.

Follow your breath in your surfing and life to scan your body's energy flows and blocks. When you feel resistance or tension walk towards it unarmed, relax your shoulders, open your heart centre and inhale deeply. Use your exhalation to explore blockages with compassion and breathe out tension like dissolving mist.

It's best not to fight resistance but to work with it as a friend or guide into your emotions. Don't be afraid. Breathe into it, lean into it and let it show you new ways. Let it reveal insights you've avoided up until now.

There are times when our surfing and our lives feel like they're going backwards. These are the times when it's even more important to show up and practice each day with commitment and faith.

It's the practice, the participation in hard times that humbles us and grounds us so that when our next leaps ahead occur (as they always do), we are all the more grateful and graceful in our renewed flow.

In surfing and in life let no wave or experience be wasted. Be curious and learn from every paddle out, every wave attempted and every wipe out. At the same time, look around you to watch those who model excellence. Study their take offs and manoeuvres, see what they do to bring their effortless skill to life. Use each session and each day as a learning process.

When you head to the surf or into your day form your intentions and give your thanks but don't hold inflexible expectations. Who knows what the conditions will be like when you arrive? The ocean is a mighty force and it is up to us to adapt to her winds, tides and swells as we find them in each moment. If we have set expectations we may be disappointed. If we are curious and form intentions that connect to the conditions, we may find unexpected insights and delights.

Time flexes on a surfboard and in life. What may be four seconds on a clock is enough time to ride a righthander from the point to the rock wall, transform a life and talk to God. It's not about the amount of time we have but what we do with it.

Let your breath take you to the centre of your surfing, to the centre of your life. Breathe deeply into the belly then breathe out through the entire body. Notice the pause between the inhale and the exhale, between the exhale and the inhale – like an eagle hovering in the breeze. There in that pause you can find peace 24 hours a day, seven days a week.

You are never too old to begin. It's never too late to start surfing or an aware and grateful life. If the yearning rises within you, honour it and begin.

Give thanks. To Mother Nature, the Creator, the Universe, the cosmos, the ocean, your kids, your partner, your employer, your friends, your enemies, yourself. There is always something to be grateful for and giving thanks brings grace and spaciousness to busy lives.

Get out of your head and into your body. Stretch your arms up to the sky. Feel your feet on the sand. Open your heart centre and walk into the world unarmed. Honour the heart's wisdom and depth. Honour the body's wisdoms and depths.

Everything changes, everything passes. The onshore winds will eventually swing offshore. The low tide dumpers will fill out with the rising tide. Winter passes and summer rises. Don't despair the hard times, they will shift and move. Don't hold too tightly to the good times, they too will pass. Be present to the truth, beauty and wisdom of each moment.

When you paddle out into the surf, don't try to force your way through the incoming sets of waves. Wait patiently for the lull when the ocean inhales and all becomes calm. Be patient and wait, because a lull will always appear and when it does then it's much easier to paddle out the back, find your place in the lineup and wait for the sets of waves to come rolling in so you can catch them.

*As kids we grow up with life-and-death warnings about staying
away from rips at the beach. So when we take up surfing it's a huge
mental leap to contemplate the possibility of rips being our friends.
Often they are the super-highways that can take us straight out the
back to the lineup without having to endlessly paddle, duck dive
and turtle roll our boards through the incoming waves.*

*Life can be like that too. We have opportunities to revisit our big
scary childhood stories and sometimes, with a larger perspective of
life, transform them into nourishment and new ways of living.*

When we take time for ourselves to go surfing, the quiet that arises inside us can quickly fill with mind chatter of to-do lists, grievances and the inner critic. It's almost as if they've been waiting to pounce at the first sign of internal silence. Don't despair! Breathe. Deep. Trust your breath to take you into peace and silence and simply let the chatter dissolve and blow away when you exhale.

There is a calculated risk we live with as surfers that each time we paddle out there is a very small chance we may not glide back in. We are playing unarmed in a space we can't control in which bigger predators than us call home.

We all know we're going to die sometime but few of us ever admit that fact openly or live with it honestly, surrendered to it.

But if we did surrender to the fact of our deaths then maybe it would be much easier to surrender into life. To disarm ourselves and walk through life more softly, more vulnerably, more tenderly, more kindly, more compassionately and more lovingly; not sweating the small or even the big stuff.

Open to the miracle of your life, this life, for as long as you are here.

We have within us a capacity to love all of life without judgement or exclusion, like the ocean. What if we are all from the one source of life, one infinite, eternal energy? Then all life is one.

The ocean accepts all in her waters: whales, whalers and protectors; predators and prey alike without judgement or exception. So too the sun and the moon and the sky. There is deeply challenging wisdom in Mother Nature.

Allow yourself to be moved by beauty. Look for the sunrises and sunsets, the big blue skies, the clouds, the forests, the sparkle of light across the sea. Gasp at the wonders of Mother Nature and let tears of tenderness flow. This life is so fleeting and precious.

Grow your awareness of the elegance of your spine, a core energy channel and the key infrastructure of your body.

When paddling or sitting on your surfboard bring your attention to the whole spine, from the tailbone to the base of your skull. Mindfully activate the muscles that support your spine and notice the energy flowing through your spine — does it move easily or is it blocked?

Love your spine as the miracle it is — the enabler of movement and mobility. Look after it lovingly.

In between sets of waves there are quiet times called lulls. There is usually a rhythm and a tempo between sets and lulls so there are opportunities to be actively surfing waves, paddling out and then resting before the next set of waves arrives.

Life is a bit like that too when we step back and see the patterns of busyness and opportunities for restoration. It's healthy to slow down and refill your wellspring when there is a lull. It's the perfect time to sit still and be quiet. To look at the beauty around you and give thanks. To rest your body and mind and breathe deeply.

Then when the next set of busyness comes as it always does, you are ready to roll with the waves. To paddle hard, be brave and surf the swell with everything you've got.

Surfing is more than standing up on a surfboard. Life is more than work or even family. They are both a deep exploration of complex, mysterious systems and a lifelong unfolding if you are open to their magic. If you let them, they will bring you meaning and depth.

Apparently, as a general rule of thumb, it takes five years of consistent surfing from the time of our basic learning, to feel comfortable in the water and on our surfboard. It takes that long to learn to read the conditions well and match your skills to the conditions. It can take 10 years to actually surf well...

This is not a sprint!

In a lifelong learning process, we earn our place in the swell and in the lineup through consistent practice, facing our fears, playing and laughing, testing and honing our skills and senses, and respecting the ocean and fellow surfers.

It's best not to define the ocean by the surfability of the swell. The ocean is the ocean — extraordinary, mystical and powerful as she is, in and of herself.

In life it's usually best not to define your day by what you achieved. Our lives are extraordinary, mystical and powerful in and of themselves too, no matter how much you got done or not.

Our judgements about what we achieve are often best suspended so that we can simply be.

Confidence is a key resource in our set of surfing skills and attitudes but we don't always feel confident out there in the big blue. Our confidence can ebb and flow like the tide.

In times when your confidence is low go easy on yourself. Treat yourself like a child learning to surf and be kind about the conditions you go out in and how you talk to yourself. If you nourish yourself in these times you will catch some waves, paddle well and most importantly, you will have fun so your confidence can return like the rising tide. Then you can begin to push your edges again.

It's just the same with life. Be kind to yourself in times of uncertainty; push your edges when you feel strong.

In surfing and in life we are powerless but not helpless.

We can't possibly control the tides, the swell, the winds or the waves but we do have our surfboards, our paddling skills, our local knowledge, and our courage to support us out there in the ocean.

In life we can't possibly control what comes at us either including loss, death and suffering. But we have our practices, attitudes, behaviours and tools that can support us. Things like meditation, surfing, yoga, mindfulness, compassion, nourishing food and exercise.

So when a rogue wave rears up at us in the ocean or in life we're not helpless, we know what to do to stay grounded, present and open.

There is much joy and bliss to be found in surfing and in life. Carry yourself lightly. Don't get bogged down in check boxes or to-do lists but learn to connect joyfully with eternal energy, inspiration and Big Spirit. Play, laugh, share, smile, breathe. Love it all. All of it. Give thanks.

Nourish your body with fresh wholefood, lots of water and exercise. Nourish your mind with stimulating, inspiring wisdom. Nourish your heart with the company of like-minded souls who genuinely support each other. Nourish your soul through meditation, stillness, silence and your surfing practice.

Craft your life mindfully as a prayer of joy, beauty and gratitude.

Seek alignment in your body, your posture, your life. Use your breath to explore the ecosystems of your body and of your life and notice where there is flow, stagnation or resistance. Without judgement, consider what might be needed to improve your alignment and flow, and in your own time with kindness to yourself, begin to call in your resources and supports. Begin to craft or renew your alignment.

Walk tall.

Surfing shows us that within each session there is a time for strength, balance, endurance, power, agility, surrender, flow, stillness and rest. None is more important than another, they all have their place.

In life, as in surfing, it's helpful to have all these skills; but most importantly we need the awareness to know when to activate each capacity and how to combine them.

The ocean, our bodies, the Earth, the cosmos are all complex living systems from the microcosm of the cell to the macrocosm of the universe. We have endless opportunities to learn like a forest, think like a mountain and flow like a wave.

When out the back in the surf and you see a large wave or set of waves building, paddle towards it fast. Never turn your back on it to try and out-paddle or out-run it in fear because you'll never make it. If you move towards it with determination and awareness, chances are you'll either be able to catch it or paddle over the top of it before it breaks on top of you.

It seems counter-intuitive to paddle towards a mountain of water (or a fearful mountain of anything in life), but sometimes it's critical to face these things early and quickly deal with them before they get nasty.

You can't out-paddle a mighty wave but you can paddle towards it and either catch the ride of your life or glide over the top before it breaks.

In surfing and in life we are host to a huge range of emotions, from fear to love and grief to bliss. As the Persian poet Rumi suggests, in any one moment we can welcome all these emotions into our awareness.

If you feel fear, notice it, acknowledge it, breathe deeply into it and before you know it, it will pass through you like a wave.

If we fight or deny our so-called negative emotions they tend to expand and cause all sorts of trouble. If we see them all as visitors as they arrive, if we acknowledge them and then release them through our breath, they become part of the landscape of our lives, not our demons.

Without fear we would not feel the joy of ease; without anger we would not feel the depths of peace.

When I enter the ocean for a surf or a swim I usually say "Good morning Mother Nature" or "Good afternoon Mother Nature" in appreciation for her gifts and beauty.

In Yoga we usually begin our practice with an intention or devotion of gratitude and end with "Namaste" — an acknowledgement of the divinity and oneness within others and ourselves.

The Hawiians use the term "Aloha" not only as a greeting but to acknowledge our connectivity, "we share our breath...we are one..."

These words give us access to the interconnectedness of our lives and of all life. They let us stand in the microcosm of ourselves and in the macrocosm of Gaia — the Earth, the universe, the cosmos and give thanks.

May we learn to use these small phrases and rituals every day with devotion.

The early bird catches the...glassy waves. Surfing can be especially powerful, glorious and life-affirming when done at dawn as the sun rises, before the wind kicks up its heels and the challenges of the day trip us up. If we surf early we set ourselves up not only to catch the best waves of the day but also to be both inspired and grounded for the day.

Practice Yoga in nature whenever you can — on the beach, in a park, under a tree. There you will find direct connection with Mother Earth, Father Sky, sun, tree, eagle and so much more. Allow yourself to be uplifted and inspired as you sweep your arms overhead to salute the sun.

Breathe with the ocean and feel the rhythms of the universe within you. Root down to rise up as you lift into Tree Pose — touching the sky with your fingertips and feeling the support of Mother Earth as you spread your toes and root into the ground.

Most importantly, stand as Tadasana - Mountain, releasing all attachments and desires through your open hands. Find the stillness, patience and timelessness of the mighty Mountain.

Very occasionally in surfing you catch the perfect wave. There's no warning, no fanfare, no choir of heavenly hosts. It's just you and the wave in perfect harmony from take off to pull out. For a mere few seconds.

The feeling we get when we catch the perfect wave is called flow and it can't be manufactured. You simply have to be entirely present, entirely in communion with that perfect wave on your perfect board with your perfect self, breathing in and out. When it's over, simply bow in thanks.

I've come to realise that fear is the birthplace of exhilaration in surfing.

The ocean and the place where it meets land, where we surf those waves of wind and sunlight energy, is sometimes a crucible. On small sticks of fibreglass or resin we figure how to get beyond the shorebreak to meet the swells as they pitch towards the sand. That in itself can be an epic journey — the paddle out, again and again and again.

And when we reach the lineup out the back there are any number of fears to breathe into. Rogue waves. Rogue surfers. Rogue sharks.

But feeling the fear and breathing into it means that like alchemy we can ride those waves and celebrate. What was fear lifts our spirits beyond the stratosphere as we dance with pure energy; with Mother Nature; with Gaia.

I've decided that without fear there is no exhilaration — they both have their place in our (surfing) lives.

When you paddle into a wave for a take off or prepare for a Yoga inversion like handstand, commit yourself 100 percent.

Base yourself entirely in your body and lose the mind chatter. Focus on breathing into the wave or into your body, look along the line of the wave or at your drishti (gaze point). Then your commitment becomes effortless and your actions will flow easily.

When out in the surf choose a couple of stable, permanent landmarks so you can both check if you're drifting (a safety measure especially on open beach breaks), and also mark the spot for sweet waves and easy takeoffs — your secret spot.

It's a little like using a gaze point or drishti in Yoga or meditation to help maintain your focus and balance.

Stable, steady landmarks can help us find our place in the big picture of life too.

We all wipe out. In surfing and in life no matter how vast our skillset, we all wipe out because we can't control everything. Going over the falls is not a pretty sight but when it inevitably happens it's safer and easier to surrender completely and relax your body like a ragdoll. Don't resist, tense up or fight the power of that mighty wave. If you have time before you go under, take a deep breath so that if you're held down or get disoriented underwater your lungs are full of air. Then let the wave take you.

When it's over you'll feel your legrope slacken and you can follow it up to daylight, air and your floating board. When you surface, take a deep breath, look around and regroup. You might have to quickly prepare for the next wave in a set to land on your head; or you might be in the clear so you can get on your board and paddle back out (or into shore, if you've had enough).

Wipe outs are inevitable for everyone. They are humbling. They help us realise we are not the centre of the universe. Through them, we can grow our resilience and our capacity to surrender.

There is an indescribable joy in getting out of your mind and living from your body in practices like surfing and Yoga.

The body knows. It has such great wisdom and as we get physically stronger and more skilled in our practices, the body seems to rejoice.

The body is an infinitely intelligent living system. It is a microcosm of the macrocosm — part of the cosmos itself. Love its full voice and jump for joy.

For many of us, the attraction of surfing lies in the fact that you can leave all your mental and emotional baggage on the beach when you paddle out. Surfing and the surrounding elements are usually too fun, too challenging, too absorbing, too dangerous, too big, too windy, too glassy, too fantastic to think about anything other than what is right in front and all around you — the ocean and waves.

Surfing miraculously offers us the eternal present.

As you feel your surf session drawing to an end the biggest challenge becomes getting back into shore. You need to decide which wave will be your last so you can draw everything to a happy, graceful close.

If the wave you catch is too good you'll want to paddle back out for another just like it. If it's a poor one you'll paddle back out to get a better one. It's a dilemma to time and pick the last wave just right.

Give yourself time for this ritual. Give yourself over to it.

And always leave a bit of energy in your tank to paddle back in just in case the last wave takes you way off track and you have to take the long way in.

In surfing and in life closures can be tricky. Give yourself time and energy to do them mindfully because they are just as important as beginnings.

Give thanks.

Every morning. Every night. Every moment.

Give thanks.

Sally MacKinnon

...is something of a soul surfer of life, diving into experiences that nourish an open heart, playfulness and peace. Her grounding practices personally and professionally are surfing, yoga, meditation and walking, and sometimes she loves a good run too. Sally understands the advice that getting published won't heal your life, but writing will and so she writes every day. She lives and works in the mountains and on the beaches of South East Queensland, Australia.

Sally can be reached via Facebook: Sally MacKinnon
email: salmackinnon@bigpond.com
website: yourfitnessfriendgc.blogspot.com.au

Scott Johnson

...is originally from Grafton. He grew up on the Clarence River and tasted the water from an early age, both fresh and salt, weekdays in the river and weekends at the beach. He has spent 29 years at sea on various craft and witnessed first-hand the vastness of nature's offerings. He has a passion for photography and aims to capture the beauty that surrounds us in and out of the water, both natural and human made.

He recently took up surfing and finds it to be a sincere challenge for the mind, body and soul. Scott relishes and embraces the challenges presented by nature and surfing. He feels humbled & honored to have collaborated on this project.

Scott can be reached via Facebook: Scott Johnson
email: scottyj1208@hotmail.com

Huon MacKinnon-Farnworth

...has been a creative soul since he was very young particularly in the areas of music, drama, photography and multi-media. He grew up in the rolling green hills of Beechmont in South East Queensland and is a happily-casual surfer and body boarder. He is currently studying Education majoring in Drama and History teaching and is engaged to his childhood sweetheart Sammy.

Huon can be reached by email: mackworth.13@gmail.com

www.ingramcontent.com/pod-product-compliance
Lightning Source LLC
Chambersburg PA
CBHW061754260326
41914CB00006B/1097